REAL TALK
—— WITH ——
REAL FIT PROS

Lessons from Wildly Successful Fit Pros
on How to Build the Fitness Business of
Your Dreams

Real Talk With Real Fit Pros: Lessons from Wildly Successful Fit Pros on How to Build the Fitness Business of Your Dreams

By Adam Berezowsky, Jim Swift, Joe Laxton, Jonathan Lautermilch, Josh Riggs, Ray Cattaneo, and Renée Lautermilch

Cover design by Farrukh Khan
Book formatting by Saqib Arshad
Edited by Renée Lautermilch

Printed in the United States of America

thesmartshark.com

REAL TALK
—— WITH ——
REAL FIT PROS

Lessons from Wildly Successful Fit Pros
on How to Build the Fitness Business of
Your Dreams

**By Adam Berezowsky, Jim Swift, Joe Laxton,
Jonathan Lautermilch, Josh Riggs, Ray Cattaneo,
and Renée Lautermilch**

DEDICATION

To all the fitness professionals who are on fire to make a lasting difference in the lives of their clients. This business ain't easy. We dedicate this book to you.

INTRODUCTION

In the saturated realm of fitness entrepreneurship, success is more than just building strong bodies—it's about creating sustainable businesses that thrive in the competitive landscape. *Real Talk with Real Fit Pros: Lessons from Wildly Successful Fit Pros on How to Build the Fitness Business of Your Dreams* is your guidebook, offering a curated collection of insights from seasoned veterans who have not just survived, but thrived, in the fitness industry.

Within these pages, you'll find the distilled wisdom of professionals who have walked the path you're embarking on. Each chapter is a treasure trove of practical advice, drawn from the real-world experiences of those who have navigated the twists and turns of fitness business with poise.

Joe Laxton shares his personal journey of transition, showcasing how prioritizing his fitness business as his main endeavor resulted in both personal fulfillment and tangible business success.

Jim Swift emphasizes the invaluable role of mentorship in the journey to success, illustrating how guidance from experienced professionals can illuminate the path forward, accelerating your growth trajectory.

Josh Riggs advocates for a solution-focused mindset, demonstrating how a relentless pursuit of problem-solving leads to exponential growth and resilience over time.

Adam Berezowsky offers a paradigm shift by focusing on community-building over profit margins, illustrating how cultivating a tribe of like-minded individuals fosters long-term success and sustainability.

Jonathan Lautermilch addresses a common stumbling block for fitness professionals: money mindset. By reframing perceptions around sales and finances, he empowers readers to approach these crucial aspects of business with confidence and ease.

Renee Lautermilch shares a pivotal moment in her career, revealing how an intentional resign process can transform transient clients into loyal advocates, ensuring repeat business and sustainable growth.

Ray Cattaneo unveils the blueprint for creating a 7-figure-producing fitness facility, breaking down the essential components that underpin enduring success in the industry.

As you embark on your journey through *Real Talk with Real Fit Pros: Lessons from Wildly Successful Fit Pros on How to Build the Fitness Business of Your Dreams*, consider this book not just as a collection of stories, but as a strategic roadmap for building and maintaining a thriving fitness business. Whether you're a seasoned professional seeking to refine your strategies or a novice eager to carve your niche, the insights contained within these pages will serve as invaluable tools in your arsenal.

Prepare to glean actionable tips, uncover hidden pitfalls, and chart a course towards the fitness business of your dreams. Let the journey begin.

CHAPTER 1

The Main Thing

How Pursuing Your Biggest Passion Unlocks Your Greatest Potential

by Joe Laxton

 The Story

In life, keeping the main thing as the main thing can be a challenge, as passions and priorities often evolve with time. This truth has been evident throughout my own journey. I've pursued several careers, each time convinced it would be my lifelong path, only to find my passions and aspirations shifting over time. The idea of starting a gym had always lingered in the back of my mind, yet I never imagined it would become a reality.

But as they say, opportunity favors the diligent. When the opportunity presented itself, I recognized it as a chance to turn my long-held dream into reality. And as with many opportunities, it came disguised as hard work. My journey began in the realm of competitive bodybuilding, a pursuit I embarked upon relatively late in life, at the age of 35. Despite my late start, I found immense joy in the science behind bodybuilding—particularly the intricacies of nutrition and its impact on physique.

With a background in financial services spanning 14 years and a foray into the world of home inspection, I found myself drawn to the gym environment, where I could both pursue my passion for bodybuilding and help others achieve their fitness goals. People frequently sought my advice on training and nutrition, prompting me to delve deeper into the science behind muscle growth and dietary optimization.

Initially, I offered guidance on a part-time basis, balancing my newfound passion with the demands of a busy work and family life. Despite the challenges, I found myself increasingly drawn to this work, unable to shake the feeling that I was onto something significant. The turning point came when my mother approached me with an unexpected proposition—to purchase a gym that was on the verge of closure.

The opportunity arose through a connection my mother had with a real estate developer who was looking to offload a failing gym and its equipment. Recognizing the potential inherent in this venture, I seized the opportunity with both hands, knowing that it was not only a chance to pursue my passion but also a way to make a meaningful impact on the lives of others.

When the opportunity to purchase the gym arose, it was almost serendipitous. Through my diligent community involvement, word had spread about my work ethic and passion for fitness. Numerous individuals suggested to the real estate developer that he should reach out to me. Intrigued by the prospect, I eagerly embraced the opportunity, despite its inconvenient timing. I was merely 32 days away from a major bodybuilding competition—a period typically considered less than ideal for embarking on a new business venture. However, fueled by my passion and determination, I decided to seize the opportunity, reasoning that the worst-case scenario would still involve me pursuing something I loved.

Remarkably, just 54 days after first hearing about the opportunity, I opened the gym's doors to the public. From the outset, it proved to be a resounding success. Despite the demanding nature of my other commitments—continuing home inspections, competing in bodybuilding, and raising a family—this endeavor quickly became my side hustle. While it initially served as a source of additional income, it soon evolved into much more.

My relentless pursuit of knowledge propelled me forward. I immersed myself in every available resource—books, podcasts, interviews, and conversations with industry experts. As an auditory learner, platforms like Audible.com became invaluable tools in my quest for expertise. I sought insights from accomplished figures in the bodybuilding, weight loss, and coaching communities, absorbing their wisdom and strategies.

My approach was simple yet effective: I learned from the best and applied those lessons diligently. Success in this field, I discovered, often hinges on a fundamental principle—following through on commitments. In a world where promises frequently go unfulfilled, I made it my mission to deliver on my word. This dedication to integrity and accountability became a hallmark of my coaching philosophy, setting me apart in an industry plagued by empty promises.

As my reputation grew, so too did my clientele. Bodybuilders seeking competitive edge and individuals pursuing healthier lifestyles alike found success under my guidance. My side hustle blossomed into a thriving business, fueled by a genuine passion for helping others achieve their fitness goals.

Many in the fitness industry struggle to retain clients and generate referrals due to a failure to deliver on promises. Constantly chasing new clients while neglecting current ones, they find it challenging to sustain their businesses long-term. However, when approached as a side hustle, this dynamic shifts. Treating it with the same level of commitment as a primary endeavor becomes essential.

Reflecting on my own journey, I recall initially overpromising to numerous clients. However, I made it my mission to consistently overdeliver, prioritizing follow-through on commitments. This dedication yielded remarkable results—clients achieving significant weight loss milestones and excelling in bodybuilding competitions. Over the years, I've helped 34 clients shed over 100 pounds each, establishing a proven track record of success.

Central to my approach was eschewing fad diets and gimmicks in favor of evidence-based practices. By focusing on foundational principles of nutrition and coaching clients to understand their motivations, I facilitated sustainable lifestyle changes. This commitment to integrity and efficacy allowed me to maintain focus on my passion and drive long-term success.

Sharing insights and strategies with aspiring fitness professionals, I've offered guidance based on years of firsthand experience. Emphasizing the importance of mastering one's craft and prioritizing client success, I've provided a blueprint for success in the industry. Ultimately, success in fitness coaching hinges on authenticity, dedication, and a steadfast commitment to delivering tangible results for clients.

In the fitness industry, many newcomers aspire to rapid success, often underestimating the importance of experience. Yet, experience remains the cornerstone of excellence. Setting oneself apart in a crowded field requires consistency, integrity, and a relentless pursuit of results. By delivering on promises and consistently producing tangible outcomes, one can distinguish themselves amidst the competition.

The landscape of fitness underwent a seismic shift in 2020 with the onset of the COVID-19 pandemic, prompting a widespread transition to online platforms. Anticipating this trend, I had begun exploring online coaching as early as 2019, gradually taking on remote clients. This shift allowed me to transcend geographical boundaries, connecting with clients globally.

Embracing the online realm, I welcomed clients from diverse backgrounds, including one from India—a testament to the vast potential of digital coaching. This experience underscored the boundless opportunities available in the online space, reaffirming my commitment to leveraging technology to expand my reach and impact.

Adapting to evolving circumstances is crucial in any endeavor. Often, it requires a deep introspection to unearth one's true calling. Despite the passage of years or even decades, that inner voice—the one that fuels our passions and drives us relentlessly forward—remains ever-present. It's the source of inspiration that compels us to pursue our true purpose, even when faced with uncertainty or adversity.

Ultimately, discovering and embracing this calling is transformative. It's the realization that work transcends mere labor—it becomes a manifestation of our deepest passions and convictions. And in that realization lies the key to fulfillment and success, both personally and professionally.

Is it hard work? Undoubtedly. Is it easy? Not at all, but there's a profound distinction between simplicity and ease. Yet, despite the challenges, it often feels instinctual, almost effortless—a calling that resonates deep within us. Some might attribute it to divine intervention, a purpose ingrained within us by a higher power. Regardless of its origins, it's a calling that demands attention, one that cannot be ignored or taken lightly.

For me, that calling was coaching. I derive immense satisfaction from witnessing the transformations of my clients—their gratitude, their referrals, their testimonials. To receive messages of gratitude from clients who have struggled with weight loss in the past, only to find success and sustainability with my guidance, is incredibly fulfilling. It's a reminder of the profound impact we can have on others' lives through our work.

As fitness professionals, we possess the power to shape the trajectory of public health in our country. Conversations with experts in various fields—from kinesiology to hormone therapy—reveal a growing disillusionment with the limitations of traditional medical practices. Many are opting to transition away from conventional healthcare systems, recognizing the potential for greater impact within the realm of fitness and wellness.

The events of the COVID-19 pandemic have heightened awareness of the importance of health and fitness. Witnessing individuals succumb to the virus, particularly those with pre-existing health conditions, has underscored the urgency of prioritizing well-being. People are awakening to the realization that longevity and vitality are not guaranteed, and that proactive measures are essential for living full, vibrant lives.

In this pivotal moment, we stand at the forefront of a paradigm shift—one that promises to redefine our approach to health and wellness. It's a movement driven by awareness, empowerment, and a collective desire for holistic well-being. And as agents of change within this movement, we have the opportunity—and the responsibility—to shape a healthier, more vibrant future for generations to come.

People are beginning to envision a future that extends beyond their own lifetime—a desire to witness the milestones of future generations, from grandchildren to great-grandchildren. This newfound awareness of longevity and legacy is driving a shift in attitudes toward health and wellness, presenting an unprecedented opportunity for our industry to effect profound change.

For me, this realization was a catalyst for decisive action. Despite my previous ventures as a serial entrepreneur, I recognized that my true passion lay within the realm of fitness coaching. At the age of 43, I made the unequivocal decision to commit fully to this path, forsaking the distractions of other business endeavors. It was a choice fueled by passion, proficiency, and a deep-seated desire to mentor and shape the future of the industry.

Embracing this newfound clarity, I found myself inundated with clients eager to embark on their fitness journeys. While the road ahead was far from easy, the path forward felt clear and purposeful. As demand for my services reached its practical limits, I recognized the need to expand and multiply my impact.

Attending a coaching conference, I resolved to take the next step—hiring additional coaches to join me in my mission to transform lives. The decision to share my knowledge and mentor others was a natural progression, rooted in the belief that true fulfillment comes from lifting others up and fostering a community of like-minded individuals.

With over two decades of experience in the field, I acknowledge that my journey has only just begun. There's a wealth of knowledge yet to explore, and I'm eager to push the boundaries of what's possible—both for myself and for those I mentor. Through collaboration and collective effort, we can achieve far more than any one individual could accomplish alone.

While the prospect of such ambitious goals may seem daunting or even idealistic, I remain steadfast in my conviction that they are the catalysts for meaningful change. In a world where small aspirations yield small results, it's the audacious goals that have the power to transform lives and shape the course of history.

I'm not interested in surrounding myself with individuals solely focused on personal gain; rather, I thrive in the company of visionaries whose ambitions inspire and challenge me. Together, we possess the power to effect transformative change because, ultimately, we each have just one life and one body. It's a sobering reality that many prioritize the maintenance of their possessions over their own well-being. This mindset urgently needs to shift, and I believe that with the right professionals, knowledge, and coaching systems in place, we can indeed change the world.

The turning point came when my wife encouraged me to fully commit to my passion for coaching. Since then, it's been a liberating journey filled with constant growth and fulfillment. The feedback from my clients serves as fuel for my ongoing quest to improve and expand my knowledge. I've invested countless hours in study, devouring books and scientific articles, yet my enthusiasm remains undiminished. Daily messages of gratitude and success stories from clients who were once frustrated or stuck serve as a powerful reminder of the impact we can have when armed with practical knowledge and a genuine desire to help others.

It's not about possessing some elusive secret; rather, it's about effectively sharing what I've learned in a way that resonates with people. Together, we've cultivated a movement—a community driven by empowerment and transformation. And while the journey ahead may be challenging, it's also incredibly rewarding, fueled by the collective desire to make a meaningful difference in the lives of others.

🎯 The Principle

In the fitness industry, possessing extensive knowledge is undoubtedly valuable. You can be well-versed in the intricacies of hormones, macronutrients, micronutrients, kinesiology, and various scientific concepts. However, true success in this field extends beyond mere book smarts. It hinges on a genuine love for people and a sincere concern for their well-being.

Having all the knowledge in the world may enable you to make some money in the short term. Still, without a deep-seated passion for helping others, you're unlikely to sustain a successful business in the long run. People have a keen sense for authenticity, and they'll see through superficial motivations eventually.

That's not to say that financial success isn't important. We're compensated for our ability to solve problems, assist others, and provide them with the guidance they seek. The demand for reliable information and direction in the realm of fitness is immense, presenting us with a tremendous opportunity to make a meaningful impact on people's lives.

However, achieving this requires more than just knowledge—it necessitates the implementation of a system. Together, armed with both expertise and a genuine desire to help, we can truly transform lives and build thriving, sustainable businesses.

💡 Actionable Tips

1. **Prioritize Authenticity and Genuine Care:** Beyond possessing extensive knowledge, prioritize developing genuine connections with your clients. Show authentic care for their well-being, and let your passion for helping others shine through in every interaction.

2. **Deliver Tangible Results:** Focus on delivering tangible results for your clients. Whether it's weight loss, muscle gain, or improved health markers, aim to provide measurable outcomes that demonstrate the effectiveness of your coaching.

3. **Embrace Technology and Innovation:** Embrace technological advancements and innovative approaches to expand your reach and impact. Consider incorporating online coaching platforms and digital resources to connect with clients globally and offer more flexible coaching options.

4. **Commit to Continuous Learning:** Stay committed to continuous learning and professional development. Invest time in reading books, attending seminars, and seeking mentorship to enhance your knowledge and skills continually.

5. **Build a Community and Support System:** Foster a sense of community and support among your clients. Encourage them to share their successes, challenges, and experiences, creating a supportive environment where they feel motivated and inspired to achieve their goals.

6. **Focus on Long-Term Sustainability:** Prioritize long-term sustainability and holistic well-being in your coaching approach. Avoid quick-fix solutions and instead emphasize sustainable lifestyle changes that promote overall health and wellness.

7. **Set Bold Goals and Collaborate:** Set ambitious goals for yourself and your business, and collaborate with like-minded individuals to achieve them. Surround yourself with visionaries who inspire and challenge you to reach new heights in your coaching journey.

TAKE ACTION

Calling all fitness professionals! Are you passionate about debunking fitness myths and providing evidence-based solutions? Join us at Reality Meets Fitness and Weight Loss on Facebook, where we're dedicated to replacing fitness myths with science-backed facts. Let's collaborate, share insights, and elevate the industry together. Join our community today and let's make a real impact in the world of fitness!

ABOUT THE AUTHOR

Joe Laxton is a fitness veteran known for his transformative impact in the health and wellness space. As the driving force behind Joe's Gym, Joe's Nutrition Coaching, and the esteemed Awaken the Warrior Bodybuilding Team, he holds a track record as a 2-time NPC National Competitor and two-time NPC Midwest Coach of the Year. Joe's influence extends far beyond accolades, having guided 34 clients to collectively shed over 100lbs and empowered hundreds more to achieve significant weight loss in the span of 2016 to 2024. With an unwavering commitment to fostering strength and resilience, Joe continues to inspire countless individuals on their fitness journey.

CHAPTER 2
The Power of Mentorship
Lessons Learned on and off the Field

by Jim Swift

📝 The Story

In December 2011, I proudly graduated from Texas State University in San Marcos, TX – Go Bobcats! Apart from my academic achievements and two certifications, my understanding of earning a living was simple: work hard. At 23, I found myself interning at the YMCA, clueless about how to monetize my skills as a Personal Trainer in Fitness and Sports.

Entering our industry, I shared a common misconception with many others – that my education credentials set me apart. But reality hit hard; I was just another employee, a mere number on the monthly schedule, and yet another face among those lifting weights. Juggling weekend shifts at a steakhouse, I realized this couldn't be my future. It was time for a new chapter in my career.

During my internship and afterward, my days were filled with supervising the gym floor, opening and closing the facility, assisting members, manning the front desk, and catering to anyone who needed help while I was on the clock. Sure, there were a few bright spots – memorable individuals I met early in my journey whom I still keep in touch with. However, what they don't teach you in certification workshops or college is the harsh reality: it's going to be tough. You enter the industry, earning peanuts, putting in countless hours, all in the hope that it will eventually pay off. But sadly, there's a scarcity of mentors willing to invest in your growth, which is why your local gym may have gone through a revolving door of a hundred trainers in the last decade.

You're not given any groundbreaking advice on boosting your sales. Sure, building relationships with members is emphasized, but beyond that, it often feels like you're badgering people into signing up for training packages just to earn a cut of session fees (if they even bother to show up). It didn't feel genuine until you connected with someone who stuck around, getting to know you as they trained. Unfortunately, many gym managers simply regurgitate the corporate spiel on what they think will drive marketing and sales success.

Nothing drains your spirit quite like constantly feeling adrift because you can't secure clients, can't grow your income, and can't break free from the daily grind of punching in and out. This led me to continue waiting tables on weekends, working 20-30 hours just to make ends meet. Seven days a week of this routine wasn't the life I envisioned for myself, neither at that time nor in the future.

Starting my journey at the YMCA in New Braunfels, TX, had one significant advantage that kept me there longer than expected: Shawn Dassie, our Fitness and Sports Director. He was the one who initially brought me on board for my internship and later encouraged me to stay for full-time employment. Shawn had an impressive background, having risen to prominence in the private Sports Training world. From being a walk-on at Iowa State to interning with an AFL team led by none other than Kurt Warner (yes, the NFL Hall of Famer for the Rams), and later holding a Graduate Assistantship with Iowa State athletics, Shawn's journey took him to California to work with Power 5 D1 athletes and aspiring professionals.

Shawn's mission as a "boss" was to fill the gap between academia and the practicalities of the workforce, a commitment he still upholds today. While he values textbooks, studies, and data, he also recognizes the importance of practical application to serve those under his guidance effectively. He excelled at helping me streamline my thought process, emphasizing the importance of mastering the basics before delving into more complex or flashy techniques. As someone who aspired to train elite athletes after college, I was clueless about how to achieve this, especially on my terms. Shawn, however, had walked that path before.

They say sports impart valuable life lessons over time, and Shawn was dedicated to imparting wisdom to those willing to learn and adopt new approaches. I respected him not only for his knowledge but also because I was eager to succeed and transition to the next phase of my life, both professionally and personally. Beyond just enhancing my performance as a coach and business generator, Shawn imparted invaluable lessons that still guide me today.

Some of these lessons have become second nature to me over the twelve years since then, ones I've shared countless times with new trainers in Fitness and Sports. Life can be challenging, and the world can seem chaotic, but showing empathy to those we serve while still expecting their best effort during our time together might just make that hour the highlight of their day. My athletes come to me after a full day of interactions – with teammates, friends, coaches, teachers, and parents, experiences that vary in quality. They hold themselves to high standards in both their athletic pursuits and academics, so the last thing I want to do is constantly harp on them for not being at their peak performance every single day.

Instead, I offer them grace and work with them to find strategies to alleviate some of the challenges in their lives. During these discussions, I emphasize that if they can only give me 60%, then give me their full 60%. I'll take that any day over someone who claims to have 100% but consistently delivers less. Building this kind of relationship with my athletes and their parents has been instrumental in retaining clients for my business, and it's remarkable to see how much these young individuals can achieve as a result.

Another key insight I've gained is that girls often respond to disappointment differently than boys, who may react positively to being pushed or even yelled at. Interestingly, Shawn never had a mentor to guide him through these nuances; he had to learn through his own experiences coaching various athletes and raising a family. Having a mentor to experiment with different approaches was invaluable. While there's now an abundance of sports psychology resources available, the ability to adapt and evolve your coaching style based on what works best is still crucial.

Nowadays, I primarily coach female athletes, so understanding how to effectively motivate and demand their best performance over time is essential.

After leaving the YMCA, I followed Shawn back to my hometown of San Antonio, TX, where we attempted some small business ventures at local studios. Long story short, while there were moments of enjoyment, the experience turned into a nightmare for various reasons, and both ventures essentially went bankrupt within three years. When you do the math, you'll realize that this period marked only the first three and a half years of my post-college life, during which I lacked a stable gym environment to grow professionally and still struggled to develop exceptional sales skills to transition away from waiting tables and achieve financial stability.

Let's jump to 2017, a time when I'd been operating under my own banner, Swift Performance Training, for a while. Over the past 3-4 years, I'd honed my sales skills, and my reputation was gaining traction in San Antonio. Surprisingly, my next mentor wasn't even from my industry. Jonathan Badger, owner of a CPA firm, was one of my adult fitness clients who trained with me 2-3 mornings a week, bright and early before the sun rose. As my business started showing signs of success, I fell into the trap of thinking I had all the knowledge I needed for smooth sailing ahead.

But those early mornings with Jonathan were about more than just lifting barbells and dumbbells. We delved deep into discussions about our respective business journeys and aspirations. Despite being incredibly bright, Jonathan shared how being labeled the "smart kid" had its down-sides over time. He emphasized that ego and pride could be detrimental to one's career, hindering them from seeking advice from potential mentors. After all, if you believe you already know everything, why bother seeking guidance?

Having such traits doesn't preclude success, but they can limit your growth potential across various aspects of life. Even if it means asking seemingly "dumb" questions, we all need mentors. Jonathan often says, "If you want to go fast, go alone; if you want to go far, go together." This philosophy underscores the importance of building a robust support network. Not everyone fits into this network, despite their success, but it should be resilient nonetheless.

And then there's humility – the recognition that while we may be knowledgeable, we're not omniscient. Don't fear being wrong when seeking guidance; it's through this vulnerability that we learn and grow. Sometimes, I've found that despite thinking I've "learned" something, members of my network have reminded me of strategies or solutions I'd forgotten or overlooked. It's a reminder that growth is a continuous journey, and we're always evolving.

Beyond business, your network should also enrich other aspects of your life, whether it's being a better spouse, parent, friend, or leader. You might not excel in every role, but having support and guidance can help you navigate them more effectively, reducing stress along the way.

Under the mentorship of Jonathan Badger, I stumbled upon my third significant mentor quite unexpectedly. At the time, my business was flourishing as an independent personal trainer, primarily serving local athletes. It was through connections like the Yale Vannoy QB Academy and Coach Devin Threat with BLOCK Offensive Line training that I began to see an influx of athletes seeking my services for their performance needs. With the start of 2018, Coach Threat began operating out of the new gym I had recently moved into, further expanding my network.

Around this period, I began contemplating my next career move, aiming to collaborate with more sports skills coaches like those I was already working with. This led me to discover Ben Nabers of Nabers Soccer Academy through a simple Google search. I reached out to Ben, expressing my interest in meeting him, and we arranged to meet at his office in the spring of 2018.

What began as a casual meeting to get acquainted and discuss our respective professions soon evolved into a deeper conversation about my business model. We delved into details such as session sizes, frequency, duration, payment systems, and packages, among other topics. It was an enlightening discussion that provided valuable insights into refining and expanding my business operations.

Certainly not what I had expected, but I thoroughly enjoy discussing business matters like this, always eager to learn something new or offer insights of my own. As our conversation unfolded, I discovered that Ben wasn't just your average soccer skills coach at the local park. He was consistently generating six-figure earnings annually while working minimal hours and securing payments six to twelve months in advance. With his exceptional coaching abilities, he had created a waiting list I hadn't even imagined was possible in our field.

But Ben's expertise extended beyond soccer coaching; he was also a sports business coach. While I was familiar with business coaches, the idea of a sports business coach seemed remarkably specific. Interestingly, this role had initially emerged by accident, much like many other great inventions.

After years of trial and error, and falling short of his own standards of success, Ben, like many others, learned a crucial lesson: sometimes, you need to get out of your own way. While stubbornness can be a valuable trait, it can also hinder personal growth. Recognizing this, Ben made a conscious effort to step back and reassess his approach. With humility, he sought guidance and began to transform into a marketing and sales powerhouse.

Ben wasted no time in applying the strategies he learned from business coaches, seminars, podcasts, and books, generously sharing his insights with others via platforms like Facebook and YouTube. While the techniques he adopted might not have been flashy or groundbreaking, they garnered attention from fellow sports coaches. This inadvertently led to what Ben describes as an "accident" – receiving emails from individuals not only seeking advice but also willing to pay him for guidance tailored to their specific business needs.

To this day, Ben has shifted away from soccer skills coaching, focusing instead on his Sports Business Coaching program, "Make Money Coaching Sports," which has benefited over 1,500 coaches across nine countries, even during the 2020 lockdowns. His transformation came about when he decided to relinquish his stubbornness and share his knowledge without fear of judgment.

Following our meeting and some valuable advice from Ben, I purchased two of his accessible e-books and began implementing what resonated with me. Months later, during our follow-up meeting, I shared my experiences – what I had tried, what had worked, and what hadn't, based on my own observations.

Thanks to Ben's guidance, I've managed to consistently generate six-figure earnings since 2018, all while reducing my workload. Since 2022, I've also joined Ben at MMCS to assist other sports coaches in refining their business strategies and breaking free from the daily grind. My goal? To help them achieve financial independence before hanging up their coaching hats.

🎯 The Principle

You should take away a few lessons from my story and the insights shared by the three mentors we visited. At the very least, let these serve as gentle reminders of some fundamental principles that can help you grow as a coach, trainer, and person. These principles were pivotal in my own personal development and in nurturing relationships both within and beyond the industry.

Discipline and structure are often touted as catalysts for freedom, a sentiment I wholeheartedly agree with. However, true freedom also comes from removing barriers that hinder us from seeking guidance, asking the tough questions, embracing humility, and being less stubborn. These qualities not only enhance our freedom within our coaching careers but also spill over into other areas of our lives. Moreover, they contribute to our integrity and authenticity as we forge connections with others, whether for brief encounters or lasting relationships. Our communities will undoubtedly benefit from such authenticity.

It's important to recognize that admitting when we don't have all the answers, lack humility, act stubbornly, or make mistakes doesn't make us weak. On the contrary, it takes strength to acknowledge these shortcomings and take steps to course-correct. Conversely, true weakness lies in staying stagnant out of comfort and convenience, refusing to evolve or grow.

Simply acknowledging your flaws and committing to improvement can catalyze transformative change in many aspects of your life. Alongside these efforts, honing communication skills – something I certainly didn't inherit from my parents – has been pivotal in my journey to becoming not only a husband but also one day, a father. Since learning from my mentors, my thirst for knowledge has only intensified, driving me to seek deeper understanding at every turn.

By embodying these principles, you'll naturally attract a different caliber of people both in your business and social circles, leading to increased happiness. Remember, it's okay to repel those who don't align with your values – quality over quantity, always.

If you find yourself struggling in business despite your knowledge, take a moment to reflect. Are you receiving adequate mentorship? Have you been shaped by mentors who have guided you over the years, as I have? Don't hesitate to embrace vulnerability and admit your shortcomings if it means finding the mentorship you need to excel. After all, it's through humility and growth that we truly become awesome.

⠠⠮⠄ Actionable Tips

As a sports coach and sports business coach, it's essential to provide actionable tips for both short-term and long-term development:

1. **Practice empathy:** Life can be tough, and disagreements are inevitable. Show understanding and compassion towards others' struggles, just as you'd want them to do for you. Holding each other to high standards while demonstrating empathy makes you appear caring and compassionate, rather than just a stern coach running a business.

2. **Show humility/less pride and ego:** Recognize that intelligence doesn't equate to knowing everything. Don't let pride and ego blind

you to areas where you still have room to learn and improve. It's okay to set aside your ego if it means experiencing significant growth.

3. **Get out of your own way:** Problems and setbacks are part of the journey, but don't let them hinder your progress. Seeking advice and guidance from others can ease the burden and help you navigate challenges more effectively. Stepping aside from your own obstacles empowers you to take control of what you can influence.

4. **Don't go alone:** We all need support and guidance from those with experience. While you're the one putting in the work, seeking mentorship and consulting allows you to approach tasks more intelligently. Knowing you have someone in your corner can alleviate feelings of loneliness and empower you to achieve greater success.

5. **Embrace adaptability:** In the ever-evolving landscape of sports and business, adaptability is key. Some principles remain constant, while others may become obsolete. Being open to different approaches and willing to pivot as needed ensures you can maintain strong results over time. Failure to adapt may result in being sidelined from the game within a few short years.

Interested in running a more successful Sports Business?

If you have been struggling to make over $3-5k/month in your business and it's sucking the passion out of coaching athletes, we would love for you to connect with us at Make Money Coaching Sports. Check out all of our helpful tips to become more profitable on our Youtube channel: Make Money Coaching Sports, or visit our website for a complimentary 6-Figure webinar and further engagement with our Business Coaching services at www.makemoneycoachingsports.com. It's time to step aside from your own obstacles and discover how to elevate your business to greater success and financial health!

ABOUT THE AUTHOR

Coach Jim Swift is a dedicated husband, sports coach, online health coach, sports business coach, and entrepreneur based in San Antonio, TX. With a profound passion for empowering athletes and adults to achieve their goals, he's committed to supporting coaches in maintaining their love for their profession. Over the years, Jim has positively impacted hundreds of athletes, adults, and sports business owners, guiding them towards success.

Stay connected with him on Instagram: @swift_results_247, @swift_performance_training210, @sportsbizmentor, and visit our website at www.makemoneycoachingsports.com.

CHAPTER 3
Just Keep Going

How a Solution Mindset Leads to Immeasurable Growth

by Josh Riggs

📝 The Story

It's 2:35 AM, and I'm navigating the empty highway during my 45-minute drive home. Just finished unloading 2000 boxes at the Greencastle Walmart Distribution Center, I roll down the window, craving the cool air against my face as I struggle to stay awake after a grueling 12-hour shift.

"I just need to make it home to catch some sleep before seeing Emily," I repeat to myself, but my thoughts are sluggish from the day's exhaustion. Emily is my first client each morning. For the past year, I've juggled my work at On Your Left (OYL) Training, a personal training business, from 7 am to 1 pm, followed by my dead-end job at Walmart from 2 pm to 2 am. Things have been looking up; I've sold 14 clients, just six shy of my freedom number to bid farewell to Walmart and pursue OYL full-time.

Pulling into my driveway feels like autopilot, and I'm unsure if I've been awake for the past 20 minutes of the drive. Stepping into my house, I collapse face-first onto my bed, only to be startled awake by the 7 am alarm. Day after day follows this pattern, blending into one another. My freedom number of 20 clients is always within reach, yet elusive. Gain one client, one leaves; gain two, and three depart. This cycle persists for months until one fateful staff meeting at Walmart brings everything to a halt.

During an early October team huddle, my boss announces a shift to a six-day workweek starting next week, lasting until the end of December to prepare for the holidays. My heart sinks. Balancing my existing commitments with four 12-hour shifts and back-to-back clients on my days off is already challenging. After the meeting, I approach my boss, desperately seeking an alternative. I explain how this schedule change would jeopardize my business. His response is blunt: "Then quit." The rest of the night becomes a blur. To this day, I'm uncertain of my thoughts, but before leaving for the day, I inform my boss that I'm accepting his offer, submitting my two-week notice.

In the ensuing months, I practically lived at Terre Haute Fitness Center (THFC), the gym where I rented space to train clients. THFC had earned a reputation as the "meathead gym" around town. It resembled the Millennium Falcon—not particularly pretty or clean, but it got the job done. One of the most challenging aspects of establishing my business was its location in one of the roughest parts of town. Despite its challenges, THFC became my home. Over the years, the gym had changed hands multiple times and had struggled under each owner. I devoted every waking moment to it. When I wasn't with clients, I was honing my skills on YouTube University or doing whatever I could to improve the facility.

After months of relentless effort, every available slot in my day was filled with coaching clients. From 5 am to 9 pm, Monday through Saturday, my schedule was packed, with Sundays reserved for program development. It was grueling, but I relished every moment. I had achieved my goal of making a living by helping others. However, in hindsight, I realized I had been severely undercharging. While I could cover my bills, there was little left over, considering the countless hours I put in.

"Have a great night, Sam!" I bid farewell to my last client of the day at 9 pm, hoping my exhaustion wasn't too evident. As I turned to leave, Jack, the gym's owner, approached me. "Hey, can we talk for a moment?" With those words, my world seemed to shatter. Jack informed me that the gym was struggling and would have to be returned to the original owner, Tom. My heart sank as I absorbed the news. He mentioned that he and Tom would be meeting the following week to discuss their plans moving forward.

In a state of panic, I spent the rest of the week frantically searching for another gym space or even a building to lease to keep my business afloat. Money—or rather, the lack thereof—was my biggest obstacle. Despite my experience in training, I was financially strapped and lacked the funds for upfront costs. No matter where I looked, I couldn't find a viable solution with my limited resources. The dreaded meeting day arrived, and my nerves were palpable. I hadn't yet informed my clients, fearing they would leave immediately. So, I plastered on a smile and soldiered on, uncertain of what the future held.

I had two consecutive cancellations that day, a stroke of luck as it afforded me the opportunity to speak with Jack. He revealed that Tom was reclaiming ownership of the business but intended to seek out a buyer. After having the business reverted to him two or three times, I couldn't blame him for wanting out. Jack mentioned that they would be closing on Monday, just four days away. With such a tight deadline, I felt utterly lost. I had nowhere to turn but to Tom.

The next day, I phoned Tom and proposed keeping the gym operational while he searched for a buyer. I argued that a functioning business would be more appealing to potential buyers and would retain more customers. Fortunately, he agreed.

For the next two months, I dedicated every spare moment between clients to cleaning and managing the day-to-day operations of the 24/7 gym. Tom occasionally brought in potential buyers, each visit leaving my heart sinking. Despite lacking funds and a backup plan, I possessed an in-depth understanding of the gym and its operations. I knew precisely what changes were necessary to revitalize the establishment. So, one evening after training, I drafted a comprehensive five-year game plan—a roadmap to transform the gym into a thriving enterprise.

The following day, I arranged a meeting with Tom. Nervous and trembling, I laid out my proposal. I confessed my financial limitations but outlined my vision for revitalizing the gym, detailing the necessary changes. Tom carefully reviewed my plan, and after what felt like an eternity, he agreed to give me a chance. I'm forever grateful to Tom for his willingness to entrust a young dreamer with such a significant opportunity. Despite his desire to move on, he extended a lifeline, a gesture that speaks volumes about his character. If he ever comes across this, I hope he understands the depth of my gratitude for that chance.

I wasted no time implementing the changes outlined in my 5-year plan. First on the agenda: rebranding. While other business owners stuck with the familiar "THFC," I knew its reputation didn't align with my goals. The new name, Dedicated Health (DH), symbolized a haven for individuals committed to living their best lives through fitness, education, and support. But a mere name change wouldn't suffice. Day and night, I poured my energy into painting, cleaning, systematizing, and renovating every corner of the gym. It had to feel like an entirely new space. After enduring what felt like the longest montage of hard work in my life, Dedicated Health emerged after two months of relentless effort.

To my surprise, progress came swifter than anticipated. In under four months, I turned a profit, began covering the rent owed to Tom, and even hired front desk staff to manage day-to-day operations. Things were looking up—I was back on track. All my time was consumed by the gym; I had no spare moments for social media or television. My clients provided my only source of news. I vaguely heard about a concerning illness called Covid spreading overseas, but it seemed distant amid my hectic schedule. That was a mistake.

Come November 2020, my eyes were glued to my phone screen as the governor prepared to announce pandemic-related closures. While other countries had already shut down gyms and health clubs, I clung to hope that we might escape unscathed. However, after an agonizing meeting, reality set in: my gym would be forced to close on Monday. Just as things were picking up, this setback hit hard.

Most businesses struggle with a 20% decrease in revenue, let alone a complete halt just months after opening. Once again, I kicked into over-drive mode. For days, I scoured for ways to continue serving my clients and reopening despite the circumstances. After two weeks of relentless searching, a solution emerged in the form of Jonathan Lautermilch. Jonathan, along with his partner Mark Zalmanoff, were launching the Fit Pro Collective (FPC), aimed at helping fitness professionals grow their businesses online. It was exactly what I needed to navigate this crisis while still caring for my existing clients within legal bounds.

With renewed focus and the guidance of the FPC, I immersed myself not only in learning but in action. Within two months, I not only salvaged what I had but doubled it. I found myself making more and helping more people with my gym closed than I ever did when it was open.

The gym closure lasted four months, during which I rebuilt most systems and processes. When the doors finally reopened, it wasn't a mere restart; it was a grand reopening. With revenue from both online and in-person sources, I expanded my team, freeing myself to focus on business growth rather than day-to-day operations.

◎ The Principle

Since encountering these roadblocks, I've not only been running that gym but multiple others as well. Reflecting on it now, there's one lesson I've gleaned from this experience, a lesson that's guided not only my business growth but my life overall. It's the notion that, regardless of the challenges that arise, one should always seek the solution rather than dwell on the problem. There will always be unexpected hurdles, and it's easy to view them as insurmountable barriers between you and your goals. For me, tackling these challenges boils down to three simple steps.

- **Step one involves identifying the most critical aspect of the issue.** For instance, when my gym closed, the primary challenge was the inability to train my clients. While the setback of attracting new clients was significant, prioritizing the welfare of my existing clientele took precedence.

- **Step two: Once you've pinpointed the primary issue, explore whether someone else has encountered a similar situation.** Learning typically occurs in one of two ways: through personal trial and error or by leveraging the experiences of those who have navigated similar challenges. Fortunately, in today's digital age, connecting with knowledgeable individuals has never been easier. It merely requires a willingness to acknowledge one's limitations and, in some cases, invest in seeking guidance.

- **Step three is perhaps the most demanding: action.** Once you've received advice or mapped out a path forward, the real work begins. You must fully commit to the prescribed process, even if it pushes you out of your comfort zone and entails following someone else's guidance. My journey through adversity was only possible because I dedicated myself wholeheartedly to the process, persevering through the difficulties, and pressing onward despite the challenges and discomfort.

I'm dedicated to being a guiding light for those navigating their own paths. While my journey in business may be relatively short, I've overcome significant obstacles and believe the insights I've gained can make a real difference for others. That's why I've begun sharing my experiences through YouTube videos, detailing what's worked for me and propelled me to where I am today. If you're seeking guidance, I invite you to explore my channel at youtube.com/iamjoshriggs and tap into the knowledge I've accumulated on my entrepreneurial journey.

ABOUT THE AUTHOR

Josh Riggs boasts 8 years of experience in the fitness industry, a journey that has seen him transition from a part-time trainer to a multifaceted entrepreneur. Today, he stands as the co-owner and operator of multiple gym locations, including West Indy Barbell and Dedicated Health, alongside his trusted partners. Throughout his career, Josh has been instrumental in guiding numerous individuals towards achieving their fitness aspirations. Driven by a mission to empower others to live their best lives through fitness, education, and unwavering support, he consistently strives to make a positive impact. Beyond his gym endeavors, Josh extends his expertise by offering business coaching to fitness professionals worldwide, all while serving as a coach for the Fit Pro Collective. Through his podcast and YouTube channel, Business Junkie, Josh endeavors to share valuable life lessons and insights gleaned from his entrepreneurial journey.

CHAPTER 4
If You Can Close Love, You Can Close Sales
by Jonathan Lautermilch

The Story

When most people think of the word sales, they envision money or a time when someone got one over on them. What I'm about to share with you is going to rewire your mindset to what sales really is.

Sales is simply persuasion.

You're persuading someone to live a better life, persuading them to make better choices for themselves, or even persuading them to buy into you and your ideas. We are all wired to be salespeople. We were built to persuade others of our ideas and beliefs—this tendency comes from our very biology.

The one force that drives us all... SEX ...

At a very young age, like most boys, my main focus in my life was to find a girl.

Little did I know, it would be through this pursuit that I would begin sharpening my sales skills.

Let me explain what I mean by sharing two stories with you about the two loves of my life who taught me invaluable lessons.

My first real lesson on high ticket sales...

Theresa was the first love of my life. I was 16 years old and a sophomore in high school when I first laid eyes on her. I was attracted to her immediately. She had brown hair, brown eyes, worked out every single day, and it showed. Now, at the time, she was way out of my league. And I mean, waaaay out of my league. I was a sophomore while she was a junior, and she was one of the cool kids at school. I had just moved to her school and was still making friends and getting used to my new surroundings.

I first saw her when we were in homeroom. I was terrified to talk to her for a month. Over the next couple of months, she awkwardly caught me gazing at her from across the room. We finally had a conversation when the teachers paired us together for a project. Through that project, Theresa gave me the opportunity to get to know her better, and we were able to hang out with common friends. This led to us being out alone a couple of times. After that, I got my nerve up to ask her on an actual date. As I sat there in terror waiting for her response, she smiled and nodded back, "Sure."

This would be one of the first sales I'd ever make, and it would initiate my addiction to winning. Funnily enough, later on, she would ask me why I didn't ask her out sooner.

It took me so long to ask her out because I was terrified of being rejected. Before her, I hadn't had much luck with the ladies.

Now, don't get me wrong. I'd dated before Theresa, but it was never like it felt with her. Before I asked her on a date, something inside me changed; it pushed me to go. I thought, *if I don't ask for it, I'll regret it for the rest of my life*. From that pitch and the courage to ask for that first date, we wound up being in a five-year relationship—and that alone taught me a boatload of lessons.

How many times have you been across the table from a client and felt terrified to ask for the sale? How many times have you met your dream client only to be too scared to ask for the opportunity for their business? Remember, if you don't ask, you'll never get your dream girl, your dream guy, or your dream client.

How My Wife Taught Me the Long Game When It Came to Sales

The second lady in the story is actually the most important lady in my life today; my wife, Renée. Renée and I met 11 years ago in a pretty funny way. We were personal trainers at the same gym. At the time, I'd been working as a personal trainer for two years, so I had a little bit of experience. But you would never know it by the looks of me or by the way I spoke. I hid it very well. When Renée was recruited to the gym by our general manager, I had an opportunity to get to know her.

Renée was recruited because she was the eye of the gym. Every staff member knew her, and all the guys wanted to be with her.

I watched each of my fellow colleagues make their pitch and bomb as they clearly overlooked the universal signs a woman sends at the gym when she wants to be left alone. Ball cap pulled down, headphones on, and a resting bitch face that could freeze hell over.

As I watched Renée reject them one by one, I knew I would have to go about getting close to her using a very different angle. When I looked at Renée, I knew this was the woman I didn't just want to be with; I wanted to spend the rest of my life with her.

As Renée and I got to know each other, we quickly found out we were both highly competitive and self-proclaimed alphas.

We didn't actually like each other much within the first month. She thought I was a cocky asshole, and I thought she was a feminazi. That's when Renée challenged me to a month-long sales contest and said she "was going to kick my ass and I was going to have to change gyms." As we competed head-to-head in that contest with the whole team watching, we were back to back, and neck and neck. I would be up one day. She would be up the next. Then as we hit the final days, she blasted past me in the numbers. I thought for sure I was going to lose and prepared to swallow my pride regardless of how painful that was going to be. As we reached the final day of the month, I was wrapping up with my last client for the day. It was a Friday at six o'clock. My head dropped, my shoulders slumped; I knew in mere minutes I was going to have to admit defeat to my adversary ... until my client saw one of our training specials. She walked up to me and asked, "What's the Buy 20, Get 10 Free special all about?"

As I tried to hide my excitement from the client, I put my arm around her and said, "That is a fantastic question! Let's go over here, and I'll walk you through it." I led my client over to the membership area, and as I looked back over my shoulder, I could see Renée and our fitness manager shaking their heads. I ever so humbly flipped Renée the bird as I walked into the sales pit to claim victory with a smug smirk on my face. Little did I know it wouldn't be the sales contest that I actually won; it would be her respect.

I tell you that story to illustrate the point that our relationship started with us not liking each other and being adversarial, but it led to common respect. We saw what the other was doing. We saw the grind and hustle we put into growing our business that month. When the contest was over, everyone won.

Our friendship led to us hanging out outside the gym. It was six months from that point until I convinced Renée to go on our first date. I don't think I've ever worked that hard for a sale in my life, but it would teach me something I would take with me throughout the rest of my sales career.

We've spent the last 11 years together, and she's my best friend and the love of my life. She is exactly who I wanted to spend my time with. Yes, it did take me six months to get that first date. If you break it down, that's a lot of sales marketing. That's a lot of good sales follow-up. In retrospect, I can see I didn't have the right offer for her when I was courting her, which is why it took six months longer to go on that first date than I would have liked. But I was resilient and persistent in keeping my eye on what I truly wanted, which was to have a lifelong relationship with her.

I'm sure you're thinking, *why is he sharing dating stories, analogies, and a sales tip in a personal development book?*

Because this supports what I shared with you earlier; that "how we do one thing is how we do everything." We're all biologically wired to want to have one special person in our life, whoever that might be. That's the origin of our sales ability, knowing that we are all designed to be salespeople. We're inherently gifted to be salespeople, so we don't just create success in business, but so we can have love and happiness. That's how we've gotten this far as a species. That's why I know what I teach works. It is built on instinct. If you can find love, I can show you how to grow your business.

🎯 The Principle

Like I said, if you can close love, you can close sales. Now, if you're a 40-year-old virgin, you may need a little bit more help than someone else reading this book. I'm not a relationship guru, but when it comes to developing relationships that turn into sales, I'm your guy.

- **This is the main point that I want you to take away after reading this chapter: you have at your disposal everything you need to sell.** You have the right instinct. You just have to be willing to tap into it.

  I'm not only talking about what you need to do to close the initial sale. What I am teaching you covers everything relating to sales, like following up and overcoming objections. Getting my first date with my wife took a lot of follow-up and understanding of what my objective would be over a specific timeframe. As I navigated those six months, I knew that my end goal was to get a date with Renée, and I also knew that was going to happen. I was very confident about what I brought to the table in terms of a relationship.

- **You must be willing to do the not-so-fun parts of sales.** You have to commit to the follow-up process. You have to understand someone's objections and how to navigate those appropriately.

- **You first have to be willing to ask for what you want, whether it's in your personal or business life.**

- **Finally, you also have to be willing to work for it.**

The Business Applications.

If you were paying attention as I was sharing these stories with you, then you can connect the dots. What I just taught you is 100% applicable to all kinds of businesses.

When I wanted to get the girl, I had to firmly understand who she was, where she was coming from, and most importantly, what she was looking for.

- **Apply this exact tactic to your business: Understand your client on a damn-near romantic level**. When you understand them, where they're at, where they want to go, and what their mental roadblocks are, then you can strategize how to provide the ramp they need to get over those roadblocks. Think about the process you go through in building relationships with your customers so you can earn their business. Is your sales process focused on getting what you want? Or is it designed to create so much value that the client truly wants what you offer? Anyone can have a one-night stand when it comes to business. The secret is in finding the clients who want to do life with you and having a process that takes them from prospect to lifer.

Once I got that first date with Renée, things were smooth sailing. With Teresa, I didn't have to follow up for six months, but I had to go on multiple dates before we got to that point.

You will also need to figure out the fastest courting system to move your clients and prospects down the path to getting into a business relationship with you.

- **Provide value and understand that that value is in the eye of the beholder**. Theresa and Renée saw totally different values in me. I had to understand that the value they saw was what allowed me to move our relationship forward.

  What is the value your clients see in you? Understand I am not asking about how valuable your offerings are in your business. I want you to know, in terms of what you do, what your client sees as valuable. I want you to know how that value impacts their life— which is where all buying decisions come from.

- **Go deep versus wide in your business**. If you haven't noticed by now, I'm much more of a long-term relationship kinda man in every area of my life. I'd rather take my time and do the work to build deep relationships with those I do business with so I don't have to constantly look for new clients over and over again.

  The same mistakes that plague romantic relationships happen in business relationships. Those looking for a one-night stand never find love. Those who quit and leave right before the relationship is about to blossom never find love. The same goes for those who are in sales. The clients looking for the one-night-stand in business have to constantly be on the hunt for the next one. But there is still an opportunity for this client to want to have a relationship with you. You just have to be willing. Salespeople who aren't willing to follow up and take part in an in-depth process to move their potential client to a buying decision will always have to wait and look for new opportunities.

When you apply a step-by-step sales process in your business, you can go deep versus wide in your prospects. When you use this strategy, you will increase your ROI more than you can measure.

Here's a scenario that provides a clear example. When you first get a lead, instead of pitching them right away, qualify them via text message or through a DM (direct message). After you qualify them, *then* you move them to a 20-30-minute meet and greet call to gain more clarity on their needs and goals.

From that call, you will have a clear idea of who this person is, what they want, and what they need. If it seems like a great fit, you can move them to a presentation call where you demonstrate the value you will add when you solve their problem.

Having a courting system in place will dramatically overhaul your business. You will need fewer leads to get the ROI you're used to.

When you're ready to start playing big and expand your greatness, Join my Real Talk With Real Fit Pros group on Facebook and sign up for my podcast Real Talk With Real Fit Pros on Spotify or wherever you listen to podcasts. You'll be able to connect with Fit Pros across the world and hear the best-of-the-best share their wisdom.

I can't wait to hear from you and help you finally get what you're worth!

ABOUT THE AUTHOR

Jonathan Lautermilch is a seasoned entrepreneur with over 15 years of experience in business development. As the Founder and CEO of Smart Shark, he is dedicated to helping 1000 small business owners grow and build lasting legacies.

Jonathan hosts two popular podcasts, "Real Talk with Real Fit Pros" and "Real Talk with Real Business Pros," and is a renowned keynote speaker on sales, marketing, leadership, and business. He is also a bestselling author and a regular contributor to publications like Authority Magazine and Thrive Global.

Jonathan's coaching has empowered thousands of entrepreneurs, and he is known for his commitment to family and faith. Based in Dallas, Texas, Jonathan cherishes quality time with his wife and daughter outside of his professional pursuits.

CHAPTER 5

People Over Profit

How Building a Tribe Leads to Unprecedented Success

by Adam Berezowsky

The Story

From 2006 to 2008, I had a real estate investment company where I flipped houses across the US. Those were tough times because it was the biggest real estate recession the US had ever seen. I worked in a small office that I rented from a friend. I remember feeling awful one day as I walked to the convenience store for my usual chips and Arizona tea. I was 80 pounds overweight, out of breath, and more depressed than ever before. It was October 8th, 2008 when I finally said, "enough is enough."

I sold my last property, scaled back my business, but didn't realize I had racked up $75,000 in debt. This low point was terrible, but it turned out to be a big blessing. That night, I went to Costco and bought a two-year membership for a big gym, and then I just got to work. Every day, week after week, I worked hard to change my life for the better.

At that time, I didn't have a clear vision for my future. All I cared about was taking it one day at a time. My top priorities were losing weight and getting my depression under control. I moved back in with my parents and spent the next year working hard. I didn't have a trainer or a workout partner, and I didn't really know what I was doing. But I showed up for myself every day and made healthier food choices. Looking back, I realize I did everything wrong during that time. I crash dieted and did way too much cardio in an attempt to sweat off the fat I wanted to lose.

Little did I know, this was setting the stage for the comeback of a lifetime. In the following year, I shed 80 pounds and felt better than I ever had before. I wanted to share this newfound feeling with the world. So, I began researching and made a commitment to become NASM Certified as a personal trainer, with the goal of opening my own gym as my next business venture. Knowing little about the fitness industry, I took a job at a big gym to gain some experience. Luckily, I worked under an incredible manager who encouraged me to develop a unique training style and reinvest in my business. Before long, I became a top trainer, with over 60 clients and sales exceeding $12,000 a month.

After about nine months of learning the ropes, I was ready to take the leap and invest fully in myself. I found a "franchise" that provided a platform and a simple business model to get started. Their approach involved subleasing a Gymnastics/Cheerleading center during its off-hours for minimal rent, sparing me the expense of a traditional brick-and-mortar location. With my location secured and a few weeks spent networking and promoting my new fitness venture, I opened my doors on April 5th, 2010. You know the saying, "if you build it, they will come"? Well, they didn't. But I did have two people sign up for my first 21-day kickstart program, and from there, I was off to the races.

Over the next two years, I went from offering one 5:30 am class to four morning class times. By the end of 2012, Groupon became a valuable platform, offering a low-barrier deal. My offer was $29.00 for the first month, and I managed to attract over 250 people. At this point, I was a one-person show, wearing all the hats. It was a bit chaotic trying to train all these new members, provide them with an exceptional experience, and then convince them to become regular members. After the trial period ended, only about 25 people stayed, but I was so nervous about using someone else's facility and having limited equipment that I offered everyone a special rate. Despite my doubts about the value I brought to their lives, I took what I could get. Over the course of that year, I ran six Groupon deals and managed to grow my client base to about 60 paying clients.

By the end of 2012, the franchise I had joined was falling short on its promises, and I couldn't see the value in continuing with them. That's when EPIC Fitness was born. I went all in on myself and never looked back. EPIC stands for Every Person Is Courageous, and let me tell you, I needed to find that courage. In 2013, I joined my first "mastermind" group, and it turned out to be the best decision I ever made. They helped me develop systems and processes for my business, freeing up my time and allowing me to create a world-class experience for my clients.

I remember one meeting where we had to build vision boards. I included a picture of a group of 100 people, a log cabin, a gym I admired, a sports car, and the logo of my new business name, envisioning it on the front of my own building one day.

This mastermind pushed me to see my business in a new light. Initially, all I wanted to do was coach clients and make a big impact in their lives. I had no idea how to create systems or standard operating procedures (SOPs) to scale beyond what I was doing. I was waking up at 4 am every day to coach my clients in the morning, then spending the rest of the day on gorilla marketing, billing, bookkeeping, and contacting leads to keep growing. My ex-wife joined me to help grow the business from just a job to a full-fledged enterprise. She was my first volunteer employee.

One of my clients, who had an incredible transformation, expressed a desire to change her career path and enter the fitness industry. She embodied our culture and acted as a leader for others starting their fitness journey with us. At the time, I wasn't even paying myself because I was reinvesting all my income back into the business. So, one day, during a conversation with her, I simply said, "Let's do this." She became my first official hire, and it was a bit scary because I didn't know how I was going to pay her. Hiring from within my organization turned out to be one of the best decisions. They understood how I coached and what I expected in terms of client experience, so it only took about a week of training before we were up and running. Finally, I had one day a week where I didn't have to coach, allowing me to focus on building the vision and future of my business.

Between 2013 and 2016, I shifted my focus to building a team that could help us grow from 60 to 150 clients. I quickly realized that to achieve this, I needed a team of rock stars who were passionate about helping others and prioritized people over profits. I partnered with the local community college and their exercise science department to create an internship program. While I found some people who were skilled at training, I also discovered that having the right personality to provide the experience I wanted for our members was crucial. Coaching and training skills can be taught, but personality is harder to change. So, I shifted my hiring process to focus solely on personality. Candidates needed to be enrolled in a training certificate program or studying kinesiology and committed to pursuing a career in this field.

By the beginning of 2015, we had reached 115 members with a team of four staff, including my ex-wife and me. Despite still coaching five days a week, we expanded our services by offering nighttime hours in a local park to reach more of our community. We also began searching for our next location with the help of a realtor, aiming to turn our vision into reality. After 14 months of searching, on April 10, 2016, we opened the doors to our new 6600-square-foot facility. It was more than we could handle at the time, but with a leap of faith, a few months of free rent, and some financial assistance from family, we made our vision come true.

During my time working at the big box gym, I cultivated a desire to create a unique culture for my own business. Over the years, I developed a passion for endurance sports, such as running races, Spartans, and triathlons. I encouraged many of my clients to shift their focus from just weight loss to challenging themselves in these races. Together, we traveled across the US, competing, cheering each other on, and supporting one another. This shared experience became a cornerstone of our culture. By intentionally facing challenges together and celebrating our successes as a community, we forged strong bonds (also known as a fear bond) that became the backbone of our community.

In 2017 and 2018, we embarked on building a Spartan Race program. We transformed our gym into a Spartan training center, complete with dozens of obstacles for practice and to challenge our members who weren't necessarily interested in racing. Spartan races became a fantastic way to foster culture and support within our gym. Overcoming obstacles became a metaphor for life, helping us break through tough times. As the leader of my business, I made it a point to wait until every single one of our members crossed the finish line before cheering them on. In 2018, we won the biggest team award at two different events, with well over 200 people setting goals and seeing them through to the finish line. The sight of "ugly cries" (the cries of success) is something I'll never forget. Whether seasoned athletes or beginners, witnessing people come together with a common goal was truly incredible.

By the end of 2019, the culture of my business had blossomed into one big supportive family. My ex-wife played a significant role in the business, but during a difficult divorce, things spiraled out of control. Despite growing the business to about 500 members and performing exceptionally, from October 2019 to February 2020, we lost about half of our members due to the situation. It was messy, involving staff and clients alike. In February, we parted ways with my ex-wife in the business, and I took on much of the operations myself. Then, on March 18th, 2020, I had to shut down the business due to Covid-19, aiming to flatten the curve for two weeks.

Completely shutting down wasn't an option. I had 12 staff members, a three-year-old child to support, and 250 people to keep moving forward while staying at home. So, my staff and I pivoted the business to be 100% online. On the first day of the shutdown, I sent out a letter offering workout equipment for home use to anyone who wanted it, as long as they kept their membership active. We provided spin bikes, rowers, dumbbells, kettlebells, bands, and anything else our clients needed. It was tough because some staff and clients disagreed with the direction we were taking, but I felt we had no other choice. Despite losing more members due to the pandemic and our efforts to keep the business afloat, we still had 120 members supporting us. The staff rallied together and delivered amazing, creative workouts via Zoom, keeping the culture alive. We hosted live spin classes, strength classes, and HIIT classes multiple times a day, and it was truly amazing.

Watching gyms close their doors permanently due to the challenges we were facing was terrifying. I wondered if we were next. Would we be able to keep going until we could reopen? Honestly, I had no clue. But we stayed strong and focused on the members who were still with us. We reopened our doors on June 1st, 2020, but had to adapt to outdoor workouts and navigate through the new reality. At the time, I was in the midst of a divorce and fighting so many internal and external battles that I don't know how I managed to pull through.

◎ The Principle

From then until now, the vision has changed, but the mission remains the same: People over Profits. We're dedicated to building a culture that can overcome any obstacle. We've created a platform for our members to grow and thrive, no matter what they're going through. Life doesn't get easier, but you can get stronger. Our clients have battled and overcome cancer, experienced loss in their families, faced family issues, and endured countless adversities. They know we're here to support them, not just to get them in shape. We help them with empathy and care, as if they were our own family. Without our tribe of people, I don't think I would have made it through the past four years.

Our tribe is incredible. Not only do we race together, grow together, and support each other through challenges, but we also enjoy spending time together. We host monthly social events at local breweries, organize hikes and runs, and our gym feels more like a clubhouse where people hang out, not just a place to work out and leave. We want to be involved in every aspect of our members' lives, watching them grow and become their best selves, just 1% better every day. Because every person is courageous.

Actionable Tips

If I were to distill the mindset and approach that led to these outcomes into just a few key focuses, these are the areas I would recommend directing your energy towards:

1. **Prioritize Building Community:** Focus on creating a strong sense of community within your business or organization. Foster connections among your members, clients, or employees by organizing regular social events, such as monthly gatherings at local venues or outdoor activities like hikes or runs. Encourage a supportive atmosphere where individuals feel valued and supported, not just as customers or colleagues, but as part of a larger community. By prioritizing community-building efforts, you'll strengthen relationships, enhance loyalty, and create a thriving environment where everyone feels connected and engaged.

2. **Embrace Adversity as a Catalyst for Growth:** Understand that facing challenges and adversity is an inevitable part of any journey, both in business and in life. Instead of allowing setbacks to deter you, view them as opportunities for growth and resilience. Learn from adversity, adapt to changes, and use them as stepping stones toward

achieving your goals. Just as overcoming obstacles in Spartan races serves as a metaphor for life's challenges, approach setbacks in your business with courage and determination. By embracing adversity and maintaining a positive mindset, you'll develop the resilience needed to overcome obstacles and achieve success.

3. **Cultivate Empathy and Support:** Recognize the importance of empathy and support in fostering a strong community and building lasting relationships. Show genuine care and concern for the well-being of your members, clients, or employees, and create a culture where everyone feels understood, valued, and supported. Listen actively, offer encouragement, and provide assistance when needed. Whether it's supporting individuals through personal challenges, such as illness or loss, or celebrating their achievements and milestones, prioritize empathy and support in all interactions. By cultivating a culture of empathy and support, you'll create a welcoming and inclusive environment where individuals feel empowered to thrive and succeed together.

TAKE ACTION

If you ever need help growing your business's culture and community, or just want to connect on a personal level, I'd love to be of assistance. You can find me on Instagram at @Epic_Courage and on Facebook as Adam Berezowsky. My gym's Facebook page is @Epicfitness805. Feel free to reach out anytime—I look forward to connecting with you!

ABOUT THE AUTHOR

Adam Berezowsky entered the fitness industry in 2009 after he was inspired by his own remarkable 80-pound weight loss journey. He is the Founder and CEO of EPIC Fitness, a premier facility in Simi Valley, California, with over 345 5-star reviews. Adam has been featured in numerous publications, including Forbes, and is host of the Becoming Epic Podcast, where he and his guests share stories of conquering challenges through health and fitness.

CHAPTER 6

Money is Just the Score of Impact

by Jonathan Lautermilch

As you go through life, you're going to experience new levels and standards you choose to live by. It's part of what makes this thing called life worth living.

When you're first starting out, everything seems to revolve around money.

Do I have enough?

How do I get more?

How come that guy over there seems to have so much of it while I have so little?

The truth is, your income is directly influenced by how you think about money.

I want to share with you one of the biggest money mindset shifts I've experienced. If you choose to adopt it, it will serve you well.

That mindset shift is this: Money is just the score of impact.

Let me explain.

The Changing Definitions of Money

When I started out in the industry over 13 years ago, money was everything. I didn't have a lot of it. To me, money meant being able to live independently. Money meant being able to do what I wanted when I wanted. Money meant being able to buy the toys I wanted so I could experience life how I desired.

Now, I've realized I don't need that much, nor do I care about "things." What's important to me is the impact that I can have on other people's lives and the lifestyle I get to live. When I started to realize these truths, sales became dramatically easier for me. What I was doing wasn't about the money anymore. It was about solving someone else's problems and seeing the effect that had in every area of their life.

If money is constantly on your mind and stressing you out, ask yourself this: *what do I need to earn to live the life I want to live?*

In other words, how much do you need to make?

What is your freedom number? How much do you need to earn to get to the point where money no longer stresses you out? Until you know that number and until you reach that goal, whatever that number is, you're going to feel like you're on a hamster wheel. You're going to feel like you're Bill Murray in Groundhog Day. If you haven't seen the movie, his character repeats the same day over and over again no matter what he does differently. Break free from that cycle, and you'll get unstuck. Once you do, you'll be able to work toward generating the income you need to live the lifestyle you want.

What Does It All Mean to You?

Reach that point where you don't really need more money, and you'll have entered the phase where what you earn is just abundance. Then you've got to find out what will fulfill you long-term. You'll need to understand what your impact on this earth is. What can you do better than anyone out there? You'll want to ask yourself these questions: *What impact am I having? What problems am I solving? What challenges am I helping people solve?*

I learned how to find these answers through a personal development leader. Bob Proctor conducted a training called the Mission in Commission.

He taught that when you truly understand why you're focused on a mission, commitment becomes a byproduct.

You can apply this analogy to a client working out in the gym, too. If they're so focused on losing weight that they're constantly getting on and off the scale every day, they're focusing on the wrong target. The people who are successful in the gym concentrate on the right behaviors and the right attitude. They show up daily and are excited about what they're doing. With each day, they get another chance to better themselves. Through that mindset, weight loss becomes a byproduct.

The same concept applies to sales and growing a business. If you get really obsessed and clear about who you want to help, and you help them better than anyone else, money becomes the byproduct of your service. When you find your freedom number and shift your mindset about money, you can stop focusing on your money and start focusing on your mission. And when you become obsessed with your mission, financial success is likely to follow.

When you focus on money, you make bad decisions.

When you focus on money, you don't keep your clients' best interests at heart.

When you have a broke money mindset, other people can feel it, sense it, and see it.

But when you truly want to help and serve people, and you're confident in asking for what you and your service are worth, sales becomes just another part of your day.

Don't forget; abundance starts with understanding this principle: Money is just the score of your impact. It's the number on the scoreboard and in your business.

The Principle

This chapter contains three principles that you can apply immediately to your business. Maybe you've noticed a theme here, but I want to make these principles simple and applicable.

If you help people by actually helping them first, you make this weird thing called money. Most people are wired to think that they have to sell someone first and help them second. But the basis of a relationship's success is value. If you add value first by doing what you can to solve someone's problem, and if you're intent on building the relationship, money becomes part of the process.

Think about what it's like to date and find your dream man or dream woman. Naturally, you will build the relationship first by going on dates.

When you spend time together, commitment is formed. The same truth applies to sales. Ask yourself, *what problem can I solve and what value can I provide upfront, so it becomes a no-brainer to want to do business with me?*

Principle number two is based on what I've built my business around. It's something we're taught to unlearn—especially in the fitness industry—when we're told we need to sell first and help people second. It's this: **Fitness has an impact.** I haven't met a single fitness professional who told me the reason they got into this industry was that they wanted to be filthy rich. They always tell me they got into this industry because fitness had an impact on their life. Fitness had an impact on their family's life. Fitness had an impact on someone they knew. It was the desire to want to impact the lives of others that inspired them to be in this business in the first place.

When you give yourself permission to provide value upfront by helping people first, they will want to work with you. You will have established yourself as someone who they know, like, and most importantly, trust.

You don't need fancy sales techniques like upselling and downselling funnels, this type of sales flow, or that kind of sales flow. People don't want to be sold, but they love to buy. If you don't believe me, check out an electronic store during Black Friday. You'll see tons of people spending money on what they want. Very rarely do we see that many people spend money on what they need.

Focus on building the value of what you do by getting people to actually want what you do. Then they will want to work with you. If you can make fitness fun and get results, people will line up outside your door wanting to work with you and your team. So, ask yourself this question if you're ever unsure about how to proceed in your business: Who can I help today? Then chase the people you can help. I promise you, the money will take care of itself.

The Business Applications

There are a few applications I want to share with you that relate to a specific mindset shift. I had to realize if I was going to lead people who sell fitness, I had to find a way to inspire them first. Then I could compensate them well enough for them to justify working in fitness as a lifelong career.

Establish KPIs—key performance indicators. We need to know what to measure that will lead to business growth. If we don't inspect what we expect, we won't know where we're going. It's just like working with a fitness client. If we're not doing monthly reassessments, how will we know the program's working? And we need to know this because if the program's not working, we have to make adjustments to get back on track. It's no different for your business.

The KPIs I've built within my organizations have always been based on the right behaviors. What are the behaviors you need to engage in to achieve success?

If you want to grow active clients, you need to know the right KPIs to measure. For example, you must know the number of people who are interested in hearing about your service and how you can help them. When you know this, then you can set appointments.

When I was running teams, I would get my team members obsessed with leads and appointments. That's because I knew, worst-case scenario, as long as we had enough leads and appointments, we would find success, even if my people were terrible at sales. Over time, I would work with them on developing the skills they needed to get better at sales. But if we hadn't been tracking the right behaviors and there were no prospects to talk to, there would have been no reason to develop sales skills.

Once you get your KPIs in order, continue to focus on the right behaviors. The last thing you want to do is stress out yourself or your team about things they can't directly control. For example, let's say you're the leader of a fitness team and you're talking to one of your team members, Bob. The last thing you want to say to Bob is, "You need to hit X amount of dollars this month, or we're going to have to do a performance improvement plan." This is another way of saying, "I'm going to walk you just a little bit further out the door."

Instead, try saying something like, "Hey, Bob, you need to focus on having X number of conversations with prospects per day." If you do this, sales will take care of itself because Bob will be focused on providing value to the prospects, which is something he can control. If we get Bob focused on conveying the value of what you and your team provide, and he focuses on consistently demonstrating value to enough people, Bob will make sales.

As Bob makes sales, his profits will increase. As Bob's profits increase, Bob will continue to make more and more sales. When you get your team to focus on the right behaviors and monitor their KPIs, you will motivate them to attain the results you all want. When they experience wins, they'll believe in themselves even more than they did before. Then they'll become excited about what they're doing, which leads to self-motivation.

Thank you so much for reading this chapter. As soon as you close it, you can immediately apply the strategies learned here to your business and start reaping the benefits.

When you're ready to start playing big and expand your greatness, Join my Real Talk With Real Fit Pros group on Facebook and sign up for my podcast Real Talk With Real Fit Pros on Spotify or wherever you listen to podcasts. You'll be able to connect with Fit Pros across the world and hear the best-of-the-best share their wisdom.

I can't wait to hear from you and help you finally get what you're worth!

ABOUT THE AUTHOR

Jonathan Lautermilch is a seasoned entrepreneur with over 15 years of experience in business development. As the Founder and CEO of Smart Shark, he is dedicated to helping 1000 small business owners grow and build lasting legacies.

Jonathan hosts two popular podcasts, "Real Talk with Real Fit Pros" and "Real Talk with Real Business Pros," and is a renowned keynote speaker on sales, marketing, leadership, and business. He is also a bestselling author and a regular contributor to publications like Authority Magazine and Thrive Global.

Jonathan's coaching has empowered thousands of entrepreneurs, and he is known for his commitment to family and faith. Based in Dallas, Texas, Jonathan cherishes quality time with his wife and daughter outside of his professional pursuits.

CHAPTER 7

The Resign Process

How Prescribing a Plan and Following Up Increases Your Resign Rate

by Renée Lautermilch

 The Story

BANG...BANG...BANG!

I resisted the urge to visibly cringe as I sat across from my client, Thalia, who was banging her head against the desk in the fitness office with mild force.

We had just completed a weekly progress check-in where we discovered that, not only was Thalia not tracking with her thirty-pound weight-loss goal, she had actually gained three pounds within the last week and her body fat percentage had risen. Needless to say, it wasn't a good check-in and Thalia was clearly not happy.

I thought to myself, *I guess this is why so many other trainers seem to shy away from doing progress check-ins—fear of awkward and upsetting moments.*

I was a new trainer in my third month—still figuring it all out—and this was the first sour progress check-in I had experienced.

My mind ran through a number of ways I could respond:

I could give her some space and leave the room.

Or, I could do the opposite and try to give her a hug...hmm, but that could go very wrong if she's not a hugger. I'm not a hugger either. Yeah, nevermind. That could just make things even more awkward.

Maybe I should tell her to forget about this and we won't do another check-in until she feels ready. No, that doesn't feel like the right thing to do either.

At that moment I decided to lean into the uncomfortability and do what my client hired me to do: lead her towards the results she so badly wanted to achieve.

"Thalia, I know this sucks. This isn't what either of us wanted to see. Can you tell me what's going on? What you think happened?"

Thalia stopped banging her head on the table and looked at me, as she appeared to consider my question.

"It's all on me at my house. I'm so busy doing everything that I just can't find time for myself. And then, I get stressed and I mindlessly snack when I'm stressed."

Thalia went on to tell me about how her husband, who was twenty years older than her, expected her to do everything around the house. Meal preparation, taking care of her three step-children, keeping the house spotless...the list went on. And this was on top of her working a full-time job.

The age gap between them had created an unspoken level of intimidation with Thalia that resulted in her bearing the load of all that was expected without ever pushing back or asking for help.

The food logging she was supposed to do had fallen by the wayside, along with the cardio and additional workouts I had prescribed her outside of our three sessions a week together.

This all resulted in a total net gain of three pounds against a weight-loss goal of thirty pounds. Thalia was visibly discouraged and we were only three weeks into her program.

"Thalia," I started, trying not to hesitate too much. "Have you talked to your husband about any of this?"

"No." Thalia averted her eye contact with me, looking to a seemingly more interesting spot on the floor.

"I'm fully confident you can hit this goal, but I'm not enough of a support team for you. You need a support team at home. You need the ability to make and protect the time necessary to take care of yourself."

"I know. I just...I can't."

"Can you be completely sure you can't when you haven't talked to him about how important this is to you?"

Thalia was silent.

I shifted in my seat and considered whether or not to ask her what I was thinking.

"Thalia—what happens if nothing changes? How will you feel a year from now? Five years from now? Ten? I want you to really think about what's at stake for you; physically and emotionally."

Thalia let out a long sigh and shook her head.

Crap. I pushed too hard. I thought to myself.

I was thinking about how to backtrack when she spoke up, surprising me.

"You're right. I'm not happy now and it's just going to get worse if I keep doing everything on my own without asking for help."

I sat upright in my chair as she continued on.

"My mom always tells me I'm terrible about asking for help. Apparently, I get it from my dad. I'll going to talk to him. I'll tell him I need him to help out around the house more."

I suppressed the huge sigh of relief I wanted to breathe, although my heart and mind were doing a celebration run.

"That's fantastic, Thalia. I'm super proud of you. I know it won't be easy but you'll be glad you did it. Let's stick to the original plan and we'll reassess again in a couple of weeks."

Thalia's eyebrows shot up. "Is that too soon?" She asked.

"I'd rather it be too soon than too late. You hired me to help you lose thirty pounds. My job is to make sure you're seeing progress, and if you're not, to collaborate with you to uncover what's not working so we can adjust it. We can't make adjustments if we don't know how we're doing."

Thalia nodded, although the concern still showed in the partial frown that had formed on her face.

"All I want you to do is focus on the actions you can control each day. Don't weigh yourself at home. I don't want you to get obsessed with the scale. Just log your food and complete your cardio and additional workouts. That's it. Can you do that?"

"Yes. I can do that. After I talk to my husband, of course." Thalia smiled and rolled her eyes.

***

After two weeks, I noticed a major shift in Thalia. Where she had lacked confidence and been unsure of herself, she now emanated confidence and a sense personal control.

The conversation with her husband had gone well. Although he wasn't overjoyed with having to take on additional responsibilities at home, he ultimately wanted Thalia to be happy and healthy. He agreed to share the load at home, giving Thalia the time she needed to focus on her fitness goals.

Throughout the course of her weight loss, some progress check-ins were astounding with others showing modest progress. We didn't overly focus on the number. Instead, we focused on Thalia making steady progress by controlling what she could control each day with her food and activity choices.

After twelve weeks passed, Thalia hit her target. And then she did something that forever changed the way I approach client programming: she bought another twelve weeks of training and set a new goal of running her first 5k.

I always programmed and prescribed for a client's initial goal, but in my training infancy I had never realized the importance of continued goal-setting in making fitness a true lifestyle.

Thalia not only ran that 5k—fast forward to today and she's completed over a dozen full marathons.

And I'm also happy to say she's still married and her husband still shares the load.

🎯 The Principle

Clients hire us to help them achieve a goal. Sometimes, that goal is easily quantifiable. Other times, it's a bit more fuzzy. Regardless of how clear the goal is, it's our job to help our clients set a goal that is as clear as possible so we can put a plan in place that will support them in achieving it.

Once a plan is in place, it's also our job to consistently track progress to make sure we're not throwing our client—and their money—on a hamster wheel. Without consistent progress check-ins, we can't know whether the plan is working or whether there are necessary adjustments that need to be made. A fitness plan without progress check-ins is akin to taking a trip without ever looking at your GPS. Who knows where you might end up?

Throughout my career, I've met and led trainers who were scared to death of progress check-ins. This fear stemmed from the belief that a lack of progress would undermine their client's faith in them and the process.

When I started as a trainer, my fear was always the opposite. I feared that if I didn't track progress often enough, I wouldn't catch a lack of progress in time to make meaningful adjustments that could get my client back on track sooner. Who buys thirty sessions to learn that they didn't achieve any progress after those thirty sessions are complete?

After my first several months as a trainer, I found that the benefit of consistent check-ins wasn't just that my clients achieved better progress in less time. It also made their progress a consistent part of the conversation, so when their sessions started dwindling, discussing resign options was completely natural and expected.

Actionable Tips

Overtime, I built what had become a naturally occurring cycle into an intentional process called *The Resign Process*.

In its most simple form, here it is:

1. **Prescribe your client:** You are the 'fitness doctor'. Your client is hiring you to take them from point A (their current state) to point B (their goal state). If your client has a weight loss goal, this is fairly simple. Prescribe a *reasonable* amount of weight loss per week to determine the total time frame. Smaller weight loss goals will typically yield less weight loss per week where larger weight loss goals will typically yield more until it gets to the last few pounds. Let's use thirty pounds as an example with a two-pound per week loss. That would be prescribed as a fifteen-week goal ($30 \div 2 = 15$).

   a. "Client, to hit your thirty-pound weight-loss goal, I recommend training with me three times a week for fifteen weeks. We'll be aiming for a loss of two pounds per week, which will take us to a total of thirty over those fifteen weeks. Like anything, results can vary so we will have consistent progress check-ins to make sure we're on track, and we'll make adjustments to the plan as necessary."

2. **Set a progress check-in schedule:** Choose an appropriate check-in schedule and set the expectation with your client during the first session. That way, progress check-ins are never a surprise. It also adds an additional layer of accountability that will help your client stay focused on the daily activities they need to engage in to work towards their goal.

b. If it's a long-term goal with slow progress, set longer periods between check-ins (e.g. better mobility and posture, conduct an overhead squat assessment every 4 weeks). If it's a shorter-term goal with faster progress, set shorter periods between check-ins (e.g. twelve-pound-loss in twelve weeks, take weight every 1-2 weeks).

3. **Never wait until the last session to discuss resign options:** Even if you have your clients on a recurring EFT program, continuation should always be an occasional part of the conversation. Not all clients have the financial means to "train for life". If you sell training by the session, your client should always be aware of their progress and how many more sessions they may need to continue forward.

4. **Make fitness a lifestyle:** What's your client's plan *after* they lose the weight? They obviously can't just go back to what they were doing before. And how boring and uninspiring is a "maintenance" phase? That's typically where people slip up and end up right back where they started. Work with your client to set continued goals and challenges each time they hit an achievement. For each new goal, you should re-prescribe them and set an appropriate progress check-in schedule. My favorite transformations are the clients who go lightyears beyond their original goal to achieve fitness results they never could have imagined for themselves.

I've seen grandmothers struggling with balance end up competing in figure competitions, and I've seen a one hundred-pound weight-loss client become a top-placing triathlete. Every client you have has the potential to insurmountably surpass both their expectations and yours. That's why we owe each person we work with thoughtful goal-setting and consistent progress check-ins.

TAKE ACTION

Want to connect with Fit Pros across the world and hear the best-of-the-best share their wisdom? Join mine and Jonathan's Real Talk With Real Fit Pros group on Facebook and sign up for our podcast Real Talk With Real Fit Pros on Spotify or wherever you listen to podcasts.

ABOUT THE AUTHOR

Renée Lautermilch is a highly accomplished learning and development leader with over 20 years of experience in various industries including fitness, healthcare, veterinary services, and hospitality. She spent most of her career in the fitness industry where she started as a personal trainer in 2009. She spent several years as a Fitness Manager and District Group Fitness Manager until navigating all the way to her most recent industry role: Senior Director of Learning & Development for Gold's Gym International.

Since then, she has co-founded two businesses; myHearingU, an online school dedicated to the education and further development of the next generation of hearing healthcare providers, and Smart Publishing, a subsidiary of Smart Shark that turns aspiring writers into bestselling authors in six months or less.

In addition to her business ventures, Renee is a bestselling author of multiple books including Leading Through Love: Throwing Out Everything Corporate Taught You About Leadership & Management and Real Talk With Real Business Pros: How To Win in a Competitive Marketplace.

CHAPTER 8

Systems, Numbers, Accountability, and Leadership

The 7-Figure Formula

by Ray Cattaneo

Before jumping in, I want to stress that what I'm about to say will only apply if you desire to have a 5-star training gym with a team and consistent company culture capable of doing high 6 figures or breaking the 7-figure mark. For some, running their own gym where they are doing most of the training and client-facing work day-to-day can still be very profitable and rewarding long-term, but if scaling to a larger team and bigger impact is what you're after, the following may be some of the most important info you hear for the near future.

📝 The Story

Back in 2010, when I first started my training career at a Snap Fitness gym in Connecticut, it was obvious to only focus on what was in front of me. Being new to the game, you had no choice but to sell, deliver a good client experience, and get results. Luckily, I had previous sales experience and had personally worked out in box gyms since high school, so that part came naturally. Looking back, Snap was the stepping stone that gave me enough confidence to believe I could make personal training a career long-term.

Fast forward about 2 years, my wife and I decided to make a move to Texas. After interviewing at many of the big boxes, I quickly realized I enjoyed a smaller setting and landed at a small franchise studio in Allen, Texas: Fitness Together. It didn't pay extremely well, but it was the fastest way to get more reps in front of clients without having to do floor hours. It was there that I first became aware of all the issues you had to deal with as a trainer in order to properly get a client from point A to point B.

Let's be honest, everyone knows what to do, but getting them to do it is a totally different story. From getting them to show up, eat properly, hydrate, sleep well, do cardio or other activities, etc., all while having conversations about life, their struggles, and obstacles in between sets hoping one thing you said turns on a new lightbulb in their heads. The opportunity? As trainers, we had the opportunity to really make an impact if you could somehow manage most of the above. The downside? It looks simple, but it's not easy... And guess what, once you manage to have all that figured out, you're getting results, clients are staying, and everything seems to be going pretty well. You logically think the next best step is management or even better ownership.

At Fitness Together, I had the opportunity to rise to management, but initially, I was just managing a schedule, running some KPIs (key performance indicators), and selling for the company. It really wasn't management, in my opinion. At the time, we averaged about 60 to 80 1-on-1 training members in a 1700 square foot space. Being the manager while also watching the owner made me constantly think of all the things we could be doing better for client retention, nutrition coaching, results, and customer experience. Little did I know what came with managing and leading all those changes.

Fast forward about a year and a half in, I took over the business and decided to do my own thing. What could go wrong? Right? Well, after taking over, I quickly realized all the little things we take for granted when we're just trainers, like the amount of planning, managing, stress, customer issues, systems, processes, marketing, leadership, innovating, and holding others accountable that was involved when truly running a business while simultaneously building a team. The truth is none of that was really in place when I took over. We had a small team, but there really wasn't a ton of consistency on client experience, how we delivered the training, and nutrition coaching was practically absent.

The first 3 to 5 years in business had major ups and downs. We had trainers come and go. We had trainers try to steal clients and open up down the street. We lost clients. We had team members who refused to buy in with our changes. We had trainers who didn't know what they were doing even with certifications and degrees. We had plenty of months in the first three years where we didn't know how we were going to cover payroll.

There were moments where I just wanted to burn it all down and close. Add to that going from "manager" to owner and having to lead guys 10+ years older than me as well as constantly trying just to hit $25 to $30k a month in revenue. And worst of all, we had me at the helm struggling to understand what was really missing... Leadership, Accountability, and Knowing Your Numbers. Trust me, if you're at that point of giving up or about to take on what can be one of the most defeating and at the same time most rewarding businesses—a training gym—listen to the people in this book, and better yet, get around people or other owners doing what you want to do. You'll thank me later :)

Ok, let's get back to the story.... Getting to a 7-figure and beyond gym requires a much different skill set than, say, 100k or even 500k. Here's what I've learned... You must consistently inspect what you expect. In the beginning, I was too focused on just revenue and being a people pleaser as a "boss" or "leader." People pleasing vs. people expectations led to poor organizational culture and lack of accountability and results where people were just walking all over me.

Not having consistent core values that we hired and fired on led to an inconsistent team with some not pulling their weight and a company culture of almost having to walk on eggshells around certain staff and even some staff having their own cliques with clients.

Not knowing my numbers or what to even measure also put us on a never-ending hamster wheel of stress trying to generate sales with a constantly leaking funnel on the backend while overspending and leading to poor cash flow management over time. And finally, failing to hold people accountable to a result or numbers put most of the staff in a stagnant career with no direction, no purpose, and ultimately led to employee turnover.

The reality: through many trials and failed experiments, I've come to the realization that I was like too many "leaders" or "owners" who are very hands-off and didn't understand that expecting everyone to know what you know or just get it just from a couple of certifications isn't scalable nor is it going to lead to the growth of your organization. I'm here to tell you, after 13 years of owning and running what is now Infinity Personal Training, a 4500 sq foot facility now on track to do $1.8 Million in recurring revenue with another location opening soon, there's a ton of mistakes and lessons I learned up to this point. Too many to list, but what I'm about to share with you later in this chapter are some of the biggest foundational keys to running a successful training gym and business.

If you want a 7-figure training gym, you will eventually have to focus on Systems, Numbers, Accountability, and Leadership to achieve incredible Results!

First up is having **Systems:**

A proven process and method, or way of doing things. A process that delivers a consistent customer experience and result. A playbook for how your company does everything for marketing, sales, fulfillment, coaching, training, nutrition coaching, onboarding and training new hires, etc.

Even if you're by yourself, you probably have some system or way of doing things for how you deliver your service. It's imperative that you start documenting how everything is done. Eventually, you must have set processes and procedures for how things are done, including how the customer experience is delivered to be followed by all in the organization.

Without systems, your business will be inconsistent, and you will never be able to delegate and grow. Systems will allow you to step out of your business and know that things continue to get done with high standards. In all honesty, I could dedicate an entire chapter to this section alone, so for the sake of keeping this simple, here are some basic action steps and How-To's.

⚙️ Action Items:

1. Outline your prospect, paying customer, and staff journeys.
2. Document the handful of processes that need to be done and by who.
3. Package everything in an easy-to-read and accessible format for your staff.
4. Train your staff on the processes.
5. Lead, manage, and hold everyone accountable to following your systems using scorecards from your KPIs and accountability meetings (more on this later).
6. Solve and Evolve: Consistently aim to simplify and improve existing systems by identifying issues and improving inefficiencies.

After dialing in your systems, you must get comfortable with **Knowing Your Numbers:**

Having a pulse on the business at all times means knowing what metrics are driving your business's profitability, team performance, and customer satisfaction to help you make quicker course corrections. Making decisions most times with numbers versus emotions and measuring weekly, monthly, and quarterly KPIs (Key Performance Indicators).

Without KPIs or numbers, you and your organization will get lost, and it eventually will lead to everyone just making random statements or even worse, possibly making up stories based in fiction versus reality because no one is simply asking... is that really true? Show me the numbers. Additionally, without this, you won't be able to set objective quarterly or annual targets to improve and grow your business and team.

No business in any industry can exist without this, so get comfortable with it now, even if you're a solopreneur at this stage. To this day, I'm shocked by how many trainers/owners don't even know if their clients are getting results, if they're profitable, and what their churn rate is. You don't have to be as heavily focused as we are; however, you certainly need to know the basics to run a sound business. If that's not you, make sure you're partnered with someone who is or hire someone to run them.

Action Items:

What KPIs should you track? There is no perfect answer here. I'd suggest picking the top 3 to 7 that you think really drive your business that can be tracked weekly, and then tracking some of the rest at minimum monthly. I'd also suggest having a scoreboard for your staff where they see everyone's sessions trained, clients lost, goal percentages, quarterly goals, etc., to foster healthy competition and accountability.

General KPIs

- Marketing Spend
- Net Profit
- Customer Acquisition Cost
- Lead Cost
- Booking Rate (what % of leads book)
- Show Rate (what % show up)
- Close Rate (what % do you sell into a program)
- Recurring Revenue (monthly contract revenue, not upfront packages)
- Revenue by program and source

- Net Revenue Lost or Gained (net changes in monthly revenue from downgrades, upgrades, new clients, and lost clients)
- Lost and Gained Client Revenue and Totals
- Attrition or Churn (% of clients lost month-over-month by program)
- Past due payments
- Email Open Rates
- Lifetime value (value of customer, based on average amount of months someone stays in your program)
- Avg Years or Months a customer remains a member by program

Client Focused KPIs

- Client Complaints or Surveys
- Client Results by Trainer or Team
- Clients not in the gym for a week or more
- Client Attendance Frequency (studies show less than 2x/week will eventually lead to cancellation)
- Clients with 2 or more No Shows in a Week
- Clients saved from cancellations
- No shows by program (month-over-month)
- Low class attendance and revenue per class
- Client Anniversaries

Staff KPIs

- Sessions trained by trainer
- Lost Clients by trainer
- Trainer Goal percentages for client's results achievements
- Quarterly staff objectives and whether they are on track or off track
- Staff Satisfaction (can be anonymous)

- Trainer Anniversaries

Now that you have systems in place and you know your numbers, you must get comfortable with **Accountability:**

Setting clear expectations and consistently communicating to direct reports or team members. Giving everyone quarterly and/or monthly numbers to hit that drive their results and goals towards the company's goals. Having consistent accountability meetings with staff monthly to measure how they're doing in and outside of the job, their ability to live your core values, results expected of the role, if they are on track or off track, client retention, etc. Giving positive and negative feedback quickly. Criticizing in private, praising in public. Being their boss not their buddy.

To create a 5-star facility, your team must have accountability and management. Too many organizations are just going with the flow and letting multiple individuals do their own thing. I'm not suggesting this is the only way to run a gym, but I know if you want to build a unique culture with consistent systems, a consistent team, and profits, this is a must. Some may see this as micromanagement at times, but consider this... can you really manage anything objectively without measuring? The answer is no. Of course, there are some intangibles that aren't always measurable; however, you must hold your people and company accountable at all times. If you don't, you certainly won't have a pulse on how your team and company are performing, nor will you be able to have predictability, and your organization may eventually have a disconnected feeling or vibe versus a cohesive one. This leads to pockets of different cultures and experiences being delivered to your customers, ultimately leading to just being another gym with a bunch of trainers versus "Insert your gym's name" – the place known for "x". Worst of all, your gym may not be profitable.

💡 Action Items:

- Do you have a way to hold each position accountable?
- Who is conducting weekly and/or monthly individual accountability meetings?
- Do you know where each staff member is monthly and quarterly from a numbers perspective (e.g. sessions trained, clients lost, client results, revenue generated, their career/financial goals)?
- Do you conduct same day/same time weekly team meetings with agendas?
- Do you have KPIs that you review weekly or monthly that steer your decisions?
- If you have a leadership team, do you have a weekly meeting to review KPIs and issues within the organization?
- Do your veterans or all stars on the team hold others accountable to a higher standard without you around?

Now that we have our systems in place, we're tracking our numbers, and we're holding ourselves and possibly a team accountable, one of the most critical things you must do, especially when leading a team, is **Leadership**:

- Always doing what you said you would.
- Expect of yourself first what you expect of others.
- Seeing ahead, Simplifying, Systemizing, and Structuring.
- Working on the business versus in the business.

- Providing clear direction and vision for where the company is going and what changes are being made and why.
- Thinking of the big picture for the organization.
- Providing tools, training, and resources for your team to learn, grow, and become leaders of their positions.
- Putting the company needs first above any individual.
- Being willing to always have tough conversations.
- Always telling the truth.
- Helping your team grow and move towards their individual goals within the company's broader goals.

It's your job to create, simplify, systemize, and structure AND/OR find people who can help you do it. In short, if you want a highly successful training gym, you have to lead at all times. Never assume anyone knows how things should be done until you have it documented, communicated, taught, tested, measured, and eventually mastered.

⚡ Action Items:

- Does everyone on your team know where the company is going, what it stands for, and what your core values are?
- Does everyone live your core values?
- Is everyone on your team clear on what's expected in their role, what numbers they should be focused on to win, and do they have the tools and resources necessary?
- Did you or someone take the time to teach and train each staff member how to execute your processes and procedures?
- Are you consistently developing your team to get better?

- Do you communicate the company's annual and quarterly objectives?
- Do you actually do what you say you're going to do when you say you're going to do it?

I assure you that the 4 components above were critical in taking us from 3 to 4 trainers back in 2012 in a 1700 sq foot facility barely breaking $300,000 in revenue to today where we're in a 4500 sq foot facility with a full staff of 15 people year-round on track to break $1.8 Million+ and about to open our second location! Whether you're a solopreneur just getting started or further along in your journey, all that matters is that you simply start implementing today and just know that we were once in that place. Anything is possible with a little grit and perseverance!

TAKE ACTION

To schedule a 30-minute consultation and receive guidance on any aspect of your business, simply email cattaneo.ray@gmail.com with the subject line "7 Figure Gym Consult." Let us know what specific areas you need assistance with, and we'll be ready to assist you!

Ray Cattaneo, CEO and Owner of Infinity Personal Training, leads one of the nation's most successful 7-figure+ training gyms. With a bachelor's degree from NYU and 15 years of experience in the fitness industry, Ray began his journey as a personal trainer and nutrition coach. After several years, he transitioned into ownership, transforming his facility into a thriving enterprise with an annual run rate nearing $2 million.

CONCLUSION

As we reach the final chapter of this book, it's time to reflect on the wealth of wisdom we've uncovered together. From the humble beginnings of our own fitness journeys to the heights of success, each page has been a testament to the resilience, innovation, and unwavering determination that define the fabric of the fitness industry.

Throughout this book, we've journeyed alongside seasoned veterans who have generously shared their hard-earned insights, revealing the inner workings of successful fitness businesses. We've delved into the nuances of client retention, facility management, mindset mastery, mentorship, and community-building, uncovering the building blocks of lasting success in this tough business.

Renee Lautermilch showed us the power of intentionality in fostering client loyalty, while **Ray Cattaneo** laid out a roadmap for building a thriving fitness facility from the ground up. **Josh Riggs** reminded us of the importance of maintaining a solution-focused mindset, and **Jim Swift** underscored the transformative impact of mentorship on our journey to success.

Jonathan Lautermilch challenged our perceptions around money, urging us to embrace financial literacy as a cornerstone of business acumen. **Joe Laxton** shared his personal odyssey of prioritizing passion, while

Adam Berezowsky championed the creation of vibrant communities as the bedrock of sustainable success.

As we say farewell to these pages, let us carry forward the lessons learned and the insights gained, not merely as knowledge to be absorbed, but as fuel to ignite our own journeys. The road ahead may have challenges, but armed with the tools, strategies, and mindset cultivated within these chapters, we are more than equipped to navigate the twists and turns with grace and determination.

Remember, success in the fitness industry is not a destination but a journey—a journey marked by growth, evolution, and the relentless pursuit of excellence. So, as you embark on your own path, embrace the challenges as opportunities, the setbacks as lessons, and the victories as milestones on the road to your dreams.

Thank you for joining us on this enlightening voyage. Here's to your continued success in the dynamic world of fitness entrepreneurship.

Until we meet again on the gym floor or the boardroom, keep striving, keep innovating, and above all, keep believing in the limitless potential that lies within you.

Here's to your success.

ABOUT SMART PUBLISHING

Back in 2021, Jonathan Lautermilch was introduced to the idea of becoming an author through a mastermind he had joined.

His mentor in the mastermind had built multiple 8-figure businesses through the books he had authored over the years.

In fact, one of these books was how Jonathan ended up becoming his client and mentee in the first place.

Initially, he was hesitant...

He pondered,

"Is this the right move for me and my business?"

"Will it work for me the way it has for my mentor?"

"If I pursue this, I know nothing about writing or publishing a book. How will I even get started, much less finish?"

And most of all, he wondered...

"Is my story even worth sharing?"

What ultimately spurred him into action?

It was the compelling evidence from his peers in the mastermind who were becoming published authors. It was just too convincing to ignore.

So he engaged a publisher and embarked on the journey of writing his first book: *Groomed For Greatness: How to Get What You're Worth as a Fitness Professional.*

Although the book was successful, Jonathan fell short of reaching bestseller status. Why? The publisher he hired lacked expertise in the realm of book marketing and business strategy.

Despite this, the book proved immensely successful, adding multiple six figures to his business's bottom line.

Inspired by Jonathan's achievement, his wife, Renee, decided to self-publish her first book. This decision allowed them to gain intimate knowledge of the publishing business, from the intricacies of manuscript development and publishing to the pivotal details that distinguish an ordinary book from one that achieves Amazon Bestseller status upon release.

After "cracking the code," they began receiving inquiries from other business owners and CEOs seeking their assistance in publishing their books and achieving bestseller status. And thus, Smart Publishing was born.

Smart Publishing boasts a 100% success rate in creating bestselling authors.

Their mission is to empower 1000 business owners to become bestselling authors, enabling them to dominate their marketplace and leave a lasting legacy.

Ready to turn your book dream into reality? Whether you're an aspiring author or a seasoned entrepreneur with a story to share, let Smart Publishing guide you on the path to success. Our proven expertise and 100% success rate in creating bestselling authors ensure that your book receives the recognition it deserves. Don't let uncertainty hold you back—take the first step toward becoming a bestselling author and dominating your marketplace.

Contact us today to learn how we can help you unleash your book's potential and leave a lasting legacy.

go.thesmartshark.com/book-publishing-homepage

Made in the USA
Coppell, TX
11 December 2024

42297147R00059